A STRE

CHRISTMAS:

How NOT To Kill Your Family And Survive The Festive Season, Using Proven Stress Management Techniques Of Top Achievers.

By David Hyner psae fpsa alam abnlp

This

Christmas...

The snow may be piling up outside, the full and extended family might have established base camp in your living room expecting you to wait on their every whim and desire at a moments notice, the credit card is having a seizure in your purse or wallet, and the dog has eaten what smells like the contents of Satan's underpants and is letting everyone know about it.

Maybe the tree is leaning in a manner that suggests when it will fall over rather than if it will fall over, and your kids have ensured that their list of preferred gifts from Santa (not Satan) has been burnt onto your memory through repeated pointing at the home shopping catalogue and going nose to the TV every time an advert comes on showing their chosen gift.

The supermarket Turkey seems to have originated from a country that you have never even heard of, and appears to be bigger than your oven…. And you are too scared to check. You just know that your cousin has got their child the "perfect" gift at ten times the cost you have been able to afford, and your parents are already wrapping your gift that you just know is the cookery book that you gave them last year.

Your evenings seem to consist of picking up cards that have fallen off the fireplace or sweeping up needles off the tree that was "supposed" to be non-dropping?!?!?!?!… and your next door neighbors lights on the front of their house makes your flashing light in the window look like a really poor effort.

There will NEVER and I do mean NEVER be enough batteries, and the noise from those toys will be enough on their own to send you to the doctors for a referral to the local secure unit. That special toy that you purchased after much online research only just made it from the Far East in time and then it did not work but worse than this was the fact that your child was more interested in the box than the toy anyway.

You are looking at your diary allocating meals to use up the food mountain that your supermarket home delivery man dropped giving him two hernias when it came to the bags containing the wine and beer, and the tipping point will be after dinner on Christmas day when you have finally washed up the last of the dishes and you drag your sorry carcass into the front room where the TV is on full volume showing "again" Chitty Chitty Bang Bang, your family all asleep hugging their over stuffed bellies, apart from the kids who look at you with expectant puppy dog eyes as if to say "what are we doing next"?

If any part of this is likely to be true for you,

this book will be your best friend over the Yuletide period.

The essential guide to managing and preventing your stress levels….

And NOT killing your family!

Acknowledgements

I wish to thank every top achiever (200+ of them I am not naming them all here but you know who you are) who so kindly gave their tips, techniques and expertise during my research.

To my many teachers, trainers and coaches along the journey I salute you all, especially Prof. Adrian Furnham, Sanjay Shah, Tony Burgess and Julie French, and Kash Gill amongst many others.

Having a faith has proven to be a great stress relief for myself so "God… if you are listening… cheers big guy! …. You rock!"

Neil Bakewell for giving me the belief that I could actually write ebooks, and for "the internet fox" (CSB) for nailing me to the deadlines.

Above all else I must thank the thousands of delegates over the years who have allowed me to test and prove many of the enclosed theories, my amazing friends who put up with me going on and on about my work, and my inspiring wife and son who keep me on the right path (most of the time).

Contents.
Page

Introduction

This book gives you the skills, knowledge and confidence to NOT become the richest person in the graveyard and survive the hectic, busy… and sometimes manic festive season.

Health wealth, through stress prevention.

About the author David Hyner and his research...

David Hyner, is a professional speaker, author, broadcaster and researcher in the area of personal effectiveness. He has conducted many years of research interviews with outstandingly successful, highly effective men and women, from all walks of life. These top achievers have included scientists, inventors, authors, explorers, sporting world champions and millionaire entrepreneurs. During these interviews, these people shared the secrets of their personal effectiveness, their thought and behaviour systems and processes enabling us to better understand how they are seemingly more stress free than the rest of us, and perhaps more importantly therefore, understand how we can become more effective ourselves.

We can gain an insight into the ways they think and behave, so that we can do the same and hopefully have more energy, time and less stress along the way.

These research interviews shed light onto the ways in which these people actually prevent stress rather than manage it. After all, why would you want to manage stress if you could prevent it?

... PREVENTION IS THE KEY !!!!

This stress prevention book gives you the tools to increase your certainty, confidence and conviction in managing and preventing levels of stress that otherwise limit your effectiveness. This book is based upon the ways that top achievers think and behave when preventing stress; it looks at the causes and symptoms of stress as well as numerous easy-to-apply methods and processes of stress **prevention**.

Why write a book about

HAVING A STRESS FREE CHRISTMAS

- How NOT To Kill Your Family And Survive The Festive Season.

When interviewing top achievers over the past years guess how many of them, when asked the question, "How do you manage your stress?" answered, "_Oh yes, I managed my stress_"?

None of them!

Nearly all of them said, *"I do not manage my stress… I prevent it… and this is what I do…….."*.

In this book we will therefore look at ways that you can use to identify what causes your stress with real emphasis on this tricky time of year, and what you can do to limit or prevent your levels of stress, enjoy Christmas more, and maybe…. Just maybe… not kill your family in the process. We will also be looking at prevention methods including a closed-eye autogenic (a visualized head to toe) relaxation process.

I hope you enjoy this book and reap the benefits of reduced stress, increased effectiveness and increased energy levels. When fully applied you could possibly expect increased levels of alertness, intellectual capacity, thinking power, energy for your personal life and/or energy for your work. Whatever it is you need more energy for, this stress prevention book will make you more effective. The techniques shared within these pages are not designed to "train you" to work with other people and their challenges, but more to help you experiment with numerous simple to use and apply techniques in the hope that you will find one or two things that really work for you.

Go on….. set yourself a goal to enjoy the festive season, stay friends with every one of your family, and survive Christmas.

Causes of Stress

In this book I am going to make an assumption. How dare I eh? Well, because you are reading this it suggests to me that either you or somebody that cares about you believes that Christmas and new year is likely to be causing you some anxiety, stress, or at best, brings out your bad side?

Therefore I accept that there are LOADS of people for whom Christmas and new year is a complete joy and that for eleven and a half Months you look forward to the two weeks of fun, parties, family, gifts, faith and festivities.

Stress can mean different things to different people.

My take on the meaning of stress is that it is a strain or pressure that can be emotional, mental, physical, skeletal, negative, or indeed, positive.

The Oxford Dictionary suggests that stress is;

"Pressure or tension exerted on a material object"

Let's first of all look at and consider just a few of the possible causes of stress. Ask yourself a few quality questions: is there anything you can do to limit or remove the causes of your stress? Where can you begin to look at that? How can you begin to limit, or even remove your stress?

There are so many causes of stress and for each of us, our stressors can be found in different causes and so are very individualized.

For example, we could look at your situation and ask does the stress come from home life, personal life, or work? or does it come from a combination of these?

Do you ever feel strained or pressured in any way by one or more of these situations?

Whilst you love your family, do you dread having to spend long periods of time in the house with them over Christmas?

At home have you got a newborn baby that is keeping awake at night and into the early hours of morning or maybe you have broken sleep patterns that might be causing you stress?

Has the present, or food shopping been left for you to do and turned out to be stress city last minute.com?

Maybe you are having a disagreement with a loved one, a friend or a family member that is causing you your stress?

Is a relationship issue within your family likely to cause friction and there is no escaping it?

Maybe it is the credit card challenge having given it a right hammering in the lead up to Christmas, or maybe an ongoing financial situation (just come into a lot of money or maybe you do not have enough money – either can cause stress) or maybe it is just an unfulfilled life - no sense of purpose?

At work, is it your boss that is screaming at you day in day out about things that are not necessarily your fault?

Is it a conflict with other members of staff, clients, suppliers or other members in your team?

Would you (at times) rather be at work rather than at home over Christmas to avoid the pressure?

Or is it about relationships?

Could it be that pets within your home are causing you stress?

… or maybe taking the dog for a walk five times a day over the festive season is your way of escaping the madness at home?

I used to have a huge friendly, but VERY accident prone Labrador dog that we all loved dearly but boy oh boy … did that dog cause us all some stress!.

Is it environment? Are you too hot and you prefer to be cool? Or do you prefer quiet and it's too noisy?

Will your normally spacious home become cramped with people, a tree and gifts, food, drink, noise? ….. ARRGGHHHH !!!!!!

Is it the car?

Is it objects, things, situations, finances, children? What is it for you?

Your relationship with CSA – (Control, Security and Acceptance).

One of the easiest things you can do to identify your areas of stress is to look at your relationship with CSA (control, security and acceptance). These three things, in the main, are the biggest causes of stress and yet they are within our control much of the time. Yes, that is right. Much of the time you CAN control or at least manage better the very things that are causing you the biggest stress… once you understand, accept, and then act upon them.

You may be asking, what have they got to do with stress? Well, what we found during our research was that most peoples' stressors could be pinned down to one, two or any combination of these three things. Control, security and/or acceptance.

People may either desire more or fear lack of control in a situation, individuals may desire more or fear of lack of security in a situation, or maybe they are in a situation where they either desire more or fear a of lack of acceptance by the people around them.

If as human beings we feel secure, in control and accepted, we tend to be happier and less stressed. Some individuals are very at ease being "loners" with few if any friends (some of those on the autistic spectrum especially so) and so acceptance might be less of a stressor for them. Others may really value the acceptance of others but truly enjoy the thrill of being out of control (thrill seekers, hedonists, drug addicts etc). And some may enjoy controlling their destiny, and enjoy others acceptance of them, yet feel very at ease in situations that others might feel insecure in. For example, some people feel secure if they have lots of money and others have no issues around having nothing at all. The stress comes when we are put out of our comfort zones.

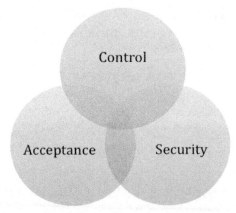

The diagram above shows the 'sweet spot' in the middle where the control, security and acceptance circles cross, and as a result we have for us the right amount of security, control, and acceptance, and therefore are within our comfort zone. As mentioned, sometimes it serves us to step out of our comfort zones, however if forced to do so against our will, this can lead to stress for most personality types.

Looking at CSA in a bit more depth – individuality.

CSA; control, security and acceptance, can be found in all the main causes of stress. When looking at the causes of an individuals' stress the reasons for their stress will be unique to them. For example, let's take physical danger, for one person the potential eruption of physical danger might be a BIG thing whereas to another it may not register on their stress radar at all.

For another person, it could just be about a control issues; for somebody else it could be control and security. For some people, they are afraid to stand up for themselves in the office and say anything to their peers for fear of a lack of acceptance.

For example, if the temperature is too hot and that person prefers to be cool, they would not say anything for fear or lack of acceptance, or maybe it makes them feel so uncomfortable that they do not feel fully in control. For somebody else it might be around the security issue, or control issue and acceptance. So, for each of us, the reason for our stress (CSA) could be one, two or three things and for every person it may be a different trigger and/or response.

Here are a few key areas or possible reasons that we get stressed;

Physical danger

When looking at physical danger, we mean if you fear being assaulted as you walk into a badly lit car park, or if you've got a job that may involve physical danger such as a fireman, police officer, or maybe a mountain rescue person. Maybe your oven is leaking gas and your Christmas succeeding hinges upon the oven working safely?

Responsibility

How does CSA relate to you within the context of responsibility? What responsibilities might you have that could be causing you stress? For example, are the whole family coming round for dinner and your kitchen simply can not cope? Are you a parent with a challenging child? Have you got a situation where you are afraid to make decisions? And you are afraid of the responsibility of decision making? Maybe you're a director of a company, or a surgeon that has life and death decisions to make.

Environment.

How about the environment? This could be the noise, temperature, lighting, or maybe your home get too crowded over Christmas or any place is too crowded or too solitary for you. All environmental stimuli at an extreme can be a stressor to some people yet not to others. I hate large city centres and love the tranquillity of the mountains or being underwater and I know others for whom, being on a mountain or under the water would be a HUGE stressor. I know some people who love and adore Christmas but can not stand their home cluttered with a tree or decorations etc. Even that "after dinner" afternoon period can cause some stress when the house has been raided of everything to eat, drink and people are sitting, stuffed to the gills trying not to fall asleep in a hot house when in truth a good nap is all they want or need.

Personality

Is there a clash of personalities or sensory styles with the people that you live or work with? In neuro-linguistic programming (often called NLP) they talk about auditory, visual and kinaesthetic personalities and how different people can be in the same situations. We could be talking in a small group of people about the same thing yet we could find ourselves agreeing with some and not with others as we all have a totally different perception of the reality in front of us. How about yourself? Is there a clash of personality or sensory style between you and your friends, you and your family or you and your work colleagues? This is especially true in families at Christmas time when maybe you are obliged to spend time with people you "love" but maybe who you would not really "like" under other ... or different circumstances.

Travelling stress

Then there is travelling stress. By this we mean either taking stress home with you from work and then taking it out on your family or taking stress to work from home and taking it out on your work colleagues. At Christmas there can be a lot of pressure to see all of your family and deliver cards, gifts or greetings in time. Maybe you have an argument with your partner, you storm out of the house and then take your aggression and frustration out on the people at work, or you go back home and take your frustrations out on those that otherwise you would never intend to? Or maybe there has been a situation at work causing you a problem and instead of dealing with it and leaving it at work you take it home with you and take it out on those nearest and dearest to you?

Leadership style

Then there could be a leadership style that causes you anxiety or conflict leading to stress; by this we mean a clash of the way things are done. If you start a new job and the job role is fantastic but maybe the leadership style of your superior or your line manager is too dictatorial or too informal for you? This can cause major frustration leading to stress. At Christmas it can be around who makes big or even the smallest of decisions. I have heard of families who have had the biggest of bust ups over Christmas, all over which film to watch, who is going to wash up the dishes after dinner, or who will take the trash out. Maybe you are a relaxed leader/elder in the home but your partner is a bit more exacting and stressed out about the detail. This can lead to tension eh?

Peer pressure

How about group pressure? Are you feeling pressure from your family to do, think or behave in a certain way? Maybe you feel pressure within your culture or as part of a business brand within a major corporation to work, think or behave in a similar way. Maybe it's when you're with your peers, your friends… feeling obliged through group pressure to think, be, or do, a certain thing or behave in a certain away. I know a few mixed race families where one family wish to observe customs around Christmas in no way what so ever, yet the other family wish to focus on either the faith side of the festive season, or the party side of it, and neither sit well with the other family and pressure is put upon that person to "be" a certain way.

At Christmas this is becoming more evident every year as parents (especially single parents) try to out-do each other with the value of gifts as if trying to buy their childrens, friends or families affection.

Interpersonal

Then there are interpersonal demands. By interpersonal demands I mean self-determined pressure - the pressure you put on yourself.

The pressure to go into debt in order that your kids get the gifts that they have asked for all year.

The pressure to cook the "perfect" Christmas meal … good luck with that one!

The stress you cause yourself by saying things like;

"I will get it done"

"I can do everything"

"I will be able to do everything"

"I will get everything done" instead of actually, "No, I can't actually do all of this, this is not good for me at the moment".

Role conflict

Then there is role conflict. Are you expected or expecting to be ding everything, staying out the way, or helping out? This could be your role as a family person versus your role at work or indeed your role at work versus your life at home. Is there a role conflict? Do you have to be a dictatorial manager at work but then at home you are required to be quite a relaxed, quiet, sensitive person? Maybe this role transfer is causing you stress? Role ambiguity and role conflict can lead to great anxiety and loss of identity. Maybe, the ambiguity of a new role such as: a new job, a new activity, attending a new school, or a new work place is a stressor for you? New demands can cause stress.

In all of those situations, have a look at, and consider, is it one of these? And if so, what are the causes?

Control, security or acceptance (CSA).

One, two or all three of these things maybe causing you stress and our internal desire to feel more secure, more accepted and more in control can play havoc with our normal behaviour. Begin to pay attention to what is going on around you and take a few moments to consider the control, security and acceptance issues that will help you determine the causes of your own stress.

Effects and Symptoms of Stress

We've had a look at the possible causes of stress so now let's have a look at the effects and symptoms of stress so that you can understand for yourself when and why you need to prevent stress and take control. Some people might state, "I need to be stressed". This is not strictly correct… as you don't "need" to be stressed, maybe you need some adrenaline pumping for you to perform physically or mentally at a higher level, but stress in itself is debilitating if it is not managed.

Very, very few situations are ever apparent when stress can help. When you have adrenaline, endorphins, serotonin, oxytocin, neuro-adrenaline all pumping around your body you might be in a fearful situation.

Let's think of an example, maybe you're being chased by a tiger- this is a stressful situation and your body needs the adrenaline to run faster to escape a chasing tiger that is hunting you down. But stress (or rather the natural chemicals released to create or deal with stress), if you do not work it out of your system, can be limiting and absolutely debilitating.

Maybe the Turkey is not going to be cooked in time and the vegetables are over done, the potatoes are on fire in the oven and you have ten friends and family sitting in the next room eagerly clutching cutlery awaiting your feast?

What are the effects and symptoms of your stress?

When you are stressed do you suffer with a lack of sleep or tiredness, are you absolutely wired and hyperactive, or lethargic?

Do you snap or shout at people for doing the things that otherwise would never push you over the edge?

Maybe even the dog breathing or the cat pushing the cat flap door open can trip you over the edge?

Maybe your heart races or feels as though it stops for a beat or two?

Does your breathing become erratic?

Notice, when you're stressed do you clench your fists, scrunch your toes up, grind or crunch your teeth?

Do you have tension in your muscles, perhaps in your neck, shoulders or forehead?
Maybe you get headaches?

What is the difference between stress and motivation?

Lots of people tell me that speaking in public, whether professionally (presentations etc) or privately (wedding speeches for example) causes them a huge amount of stress not only at the time, but at times during the preceding weeks and months.

My question to these people is always, "is the 'motivation' to give a fantastic speech greater than the 'fear/ stress' of giving the speech". If so then you are more likely to overcome your stress.

Motivation is an enabler, even if it is stress related, or as it is sometimes called, positive stress. The football team playing in the cup final can be stressed, excited, anxious, and any number of emotions and for some of them (hopefully all of them) the motivation to win the cup final, despite causing them stress, is positive enough motivation to give their all during the game. Those who become too stressed might freeze or become paralysed with fear.

Do you feel pressured (stressed) or motivated and inspired to do things?

When looking at the difference between stress and motivation, for example, if you need to overcome a fear of speaking in public and the associated stress this brings, you may feel stressed and yet you want to give that presentation (for example a wedding speech) but you do not 'have' to do that speech. The stress created might be 'bigger' than your motivation to speak and therefore as a result your nerves might limit the quality of your delivery. In this situation, stress is not a motivator however for someone else the motivation to deliver a good wedding speech may over-ride the stress of delivering it.

The desire to do a great job **MUST** be greater than the fear of getting it wrong.

Cooking the Christmas dinner can be made a much more relaxing experience if your focus is on the preparation, laying of the table, cooking and clearing up was a whole family experience and fun was had whilst doing the work. The focus could be on the fun experience rather than the fear of dinner going wrong.

People mistakenly think that they have to be stressed to do something well or get something done.

An example maybe when someone feels that they are better leaving a work project until the last minute rather than planning time through the weeks preceding the dead line. They may get it done last minute, however much less stress might occur if they had done the task earlier in time.

To re-cap:
Look at – and understand - why you're stressed, understand why you are stressed. Look at the effects and the symptoms of your stress.

Thought processes and their impact on your levels of stress.

As you think about day to day things, emotions are managed by the 'Amygdala' within the brain. The Amygdala is a tiny, almond sized and shaped, mass of neurons and electrons deep within the brain which controls your emotional state. It tells your brain how to respond to emotions whether they are true or false.

By that I mean, you could be watching a scary movie and even though the werewolf in the scary movie is not real, you can still feel stressed, anxious, afraid, your heart may pump, your breathing may become short and pronounced, you may have sweaty palms, a dry mouth, your hands maybe white as your knuckles grip the chair arms.

All these things can happen ... yet the werewolf is not real.
 So, your thoughts, in this example a scary wolf, could have led to emotions being created which led to the brain processing physical reactions to cope with the situation (eg fight or flight response).

This is something called PNI; Psycho- Neuro Immunology.

PNI is the effect of your thoughts, whether conscious or subconscious, on your emotions and your physical reactions. Basically, it is your subconscious mind talking to your brain, which in turn controls your immune system and your physiology. That is about as scientific as we are going to get here but there is plenty more information about this available should you wish to research it.

Now let's take a look at some other minor and debilitating things that cause these effects and symptoms. Some of the symptoms that you experience maybe very minor, others could be absolutely debilitating. If left unchecked, these symptoms may develop to be many times worse than they need to be. The great news is that most of these symptoms can be prevented quite easily.

Your blood pressure, sleep patterns (or lack of sleep), muscle fatigue; all of these things can be prevented and managed effectively, and all will be revealed later in this book. If not managed they can lead to all sorts of health problems that can affect your personal life, your finances, your work-life, your self-esteem, your emotional or mental well-being, or even your physical well-being. They can lead to not being able to use machinery, or drive or even have children. It can affect your love life. All of these things can be prevented.

We've looked at the causes, effects and the symptoms of stress, next let's look at some easy to apply stress prevention techniques.

Stress "Prevention" techniques.

The stress prevention techniques that we are going to look at in this book are stress prevention techniques that are applied by successful and highly effective people. These techniques have been gathered during the two hundred or more interviews I have undertaken with successful people. The successful people I interviewed seemed to have endless energy and yet all they said they did (most of the time) was think and behave more effectively than the rest of us.

Some of these techniques may appear just a little bit crazy to you. All I'll say is, I was given these techniques from very successful people, these techniques work for them, so all I ask you to do, is see if they work for you.

Have a go, please don't just dismiss them as crazy nonsense. Have a go and see if they work for you. If you feel like dismissing them ask yourself this question, if top achievers do the techniques that I am giving you here, who has got it right, us or them? When given new information that seems strange or different, it can be far too easy to dismiss it as being ridiculous or simplistic without even trying it out. Sometimes we dismiss things straight away rather than risking the remote possibility of them not working or making us look a little foolish. Well, I'm going to ask you to give 100% when trying these techniques so that you can truly see if any of the techniques that follow can help you.

When I work with chief executives and leadership teams on wellbeing, they frequently look at each other mockingly to begin with but by the end of the session having applied these techniques they are "more than sold on the ideas" and can usually identify one or two that REALLY work for them.

From personal experience I have found them to work for myself as when I was younger I used to really, really struggle with sleeping. I used to get very stressed, in fact my stress was so bad it even led to irritable bowel syndrome and all other sorts of other conditions, but now, since learning and applying these stress prevention techniques, whenever our little boy allows me, I sleep absolutely fine – just ask my wife!

It is about making these things (techniques) a habit and you can make them a habit by practicing them so that you can let go of stress. In fact, if you do everything written here to prevent stress for 21 days or more it can become a very positive habit indeed.

Now, I don't want to give you the idea that everything is perfect for me because I apply these techniques, far from it. I still have situations and some rather unhelpful "stuff" going on from time to time that can cause great levels of stress.

The thing is this, when these techniques become a habit for you they become part of you, and it becomes easier and easier to prevent or let go of stress rather than manage it and hold onto it like most people do.

You can eventually reach a stage where you might be able to relax anywhere, anytime. Yes, allow me to reiterate that, you could be able to relax anywhere and at any time. I tested this once to calm myself down at a football cup final when my team had a penalty and I was so anxious that I felt my heart was going to jump out of my chest. Even in this highly charged atmosphere with the many thousands of people screaming, chanting and singing around me I was able to help myself to take control again.

Now, before anyone goes "ugh..... NO WAY !", I promise you, I have (for charity) been in a huge aquarium tank full of sharks, barracudas and Moray eels, and I promise you that my heart was beating out of my chest but using stress prevention techniques I was able to relax myself and as a result I enjoyed the experience far more than I otherwise would have done.

What situations occur within your life that if you were able to prevent stress in the moment, you could be more effective? Maybe a disciplinary hearing? Maybe the board meeting? Maybe the sales appointment?

Or it maybe the situation you need to address at home?
Could you be more effective and conduct it to gain a better outcome if you were preventing your stress rather than managing it?

As a professional speaker I work within corporate events, conferences and conventions, I work with corporate teams, and go into schools to work with both students and teachers.

Taking into account all of these environments, the most challenging event for myself is working with young adults and teenagers in high schools, sixth-forms, colleges and universities.

Why? Because they are fearless, and yet they will sense fear in you and many will absolutely go for the jugular if they do. This could be a great cause of stress if I allow it to be so.

So, I choose to take control, I do not allow it to effect me, I take control by using some of the prevention techniques described below.

Before we go deeper into a few really useful techniques that can prevent stress in any part of your life, here is a short list of twenty simple things that we can do to make Christmas more fun, more relaxed and a lot less stressful for you and your family.

1 – get wrapping paper, tape, ribbon in the new year sales so that you have a big supply for next year at reduced rates.

2 – write a gift list so you know who you are buying for, and what you want to get them. This avoids too many forgotten relations and can be done well in advance.

"This year,, EVERYONE is getting a tree!"

3 – plan to buy gifts, make gifts or do something different altogether. One year just to be different my wife and I made spicy pickled onions and other pickles. It was really inexpensive and our friends and family liked them so much that they returned the jars asking for the same again next year. Sometimes a lot of thought for each person can be great fun as you buy or make a gift just for that person. Maybe you are not going to buy gifts this year other than for close family and instead wish to donate money to a good cause or charity. Spread the purchase of gifts over the year and as you buy them put them away in a draw or somewhere safe. This also enables you to take advantage of seasonal sales and maybe get a few each Month to spread the workload and the cost. Now there's a WIN !

4 – plan your menu well in advance and do anything and everything you can in advance to minimise your workload on the day. Get others to help out by having specific roles or jobs towards the big day and maybe even bring a starter, or main course or deserts with them. Maybe the kids lay the table, the men or ladies cook and the others clear away afterwards and wash up the dishes. How about breaking with tradition and having a novelty menu, or themed menu, murder mystery Christmas etc

5 – plan time out for you to relax, get fresh air, exercise or do a hobby. Make sure that you all get time for yourselves.

6 – maybe get family to help over the festivities with cleaning the house or maybe even get cleaners in?

7 – as hard as it can be to be strong at these times, try not to eat or drink "too much" or if you do make sure that it is only for one day then return to normal sized meals and drinking etc.

8 – aim for fun and not perfection. Roll with any challenges and apply the techniques in this book to prevent rather than manage or cure stress once it has arisen.

9 – if there are any underlying family issues or challenges try to resolve them before Christmas so that stress levels are lower to start with.

10 – if decorating the house is not your thing maybe do one room REALLY well and leave the rest of the home as it is?

11 – if you can not visit family or friends (or do not want to), plan well in advance and maybe go and visit them before or after the festive season to ensure that everyone has been made to feel taken care of.

12 – to save money and stress on sending Christmas cards maybe make a family video or photo story and send that instead or maybe write a handwritten letter which costs less, and despite taking more time in advance, makes the recipient feel very special indeed.

13 – allow time for sleeping, napping, prayer or meditation or something that stills your mind for a while to calm the nerves.

14 – do something for others instead….. Andy Browne (a great friend of mine) and his family gave up their Christmas last year to organise, cook and serve Christmas dinner to one hundred local people identified as being lonely or in need at a local church hall. "WOW !"

15 – plan Christmas with your family so you have all agreed on how things will pan out over the period.

16 – avoid the stress altogether and go on holiday for the week maybe returning to host a house party for everyone?

17 – even if you do not have a religious belief, take time to remember what it is REALLY all about?

18 – never be lonely … if you live alone, or are a single parent, or elderly, make sure that you organise meetings, friends to pop round, gatherings or outings to ensure that your happiness and well being is cared for.

19 – do something crazy … go and have an experience that you can look forward to (or escape to). This can be as crazy as wild swimming in open water with an organised group or maybe calling in on the frail and vulnerable in your street.

Or it can be a planned trip out. I used to love Boxing Day (the day after Christmas) where I used to have cold Turkey meat with bubble and squeak for lunch followed by the pub for a beer with friends then off to a football match.

Simple treat but I so looked forward tot hat day every year. For those who do not know, bubble and squeak is left over vegetables and potato mashed up together and fried as a large potato and vegetable style fritter.

20 – show gratitude at every opportunity… if you are feeling stressed, anxious or lonely it can be a great idea to press pause on your life for a short while and focus on what you have in your life to be grateful for. Being alive, healthy, friends, family, gifts, a job, a future, another year to plan Christmas?!

Lets now focus on a few proven techniques from the top achievers…

Technique 1 – a short closed eye exercise.

For the first technique we're going to do a short closed eye exercise. Before we do this I want you to think about how you hear other peoples voices in your head.

By this I mean when other people speak to you, do you always believe everything they say? You probably don't, yet we tend to believe our own voice (self talk) regardless of it telling us good things or bad things. So, if you were to hear a voice guiding you to a place of total relaxation, you might be more inclined to go with it, if the voice was your own.

Using your mobile phone, computer, digital voice recorder, or cassette recorder (do they even still make these nowadays?) I ask you to take some time and record your own voice in a slow relaxed tone, as many times as it takes until you capture one that works for you. When you are recording be sure to read the script (below) exactly (word for word), and pick a quiet room and time of day to do the recording so you don't get the dog barking, phone ringing, or doorbell chine going during the recording. If you still have any doubts at all using your own voice I would suggest you to go and see a relaxation coach or buy a guided relaxation audio to use.

Now, if anyone suffers with epilepsy, please keep your eyes open at all times (of course you may blink), and if your condition is anything more than very mild, or if you have "any" medical condition that might not be suitable for this process, I would strongly suggest that you consult your doctor before doing any closed eye relaxation process. This includes, but is not limited to, heart conditions, blood pressure issues, emotional or psychological challenges, lung or chest health issues or fits/seizures of any type. For everybody else, the outcome will be far more beneficial when you close your eyes when you listen back to the audio I am asking you to record. So, if you're driving, pull over, don't do this whilst driving or operating any kind of machinery or device.

What I'd like you to do is to find a comfortable chair to sit in. Sit up straight with your back flat against the back of a chair or even lie down on the bed or the floor if this is more comfortable or relaxing for you. If you sit in a chair make sure your feet are planted flat on the ground or raised in a comfortable manner and that your hands are placed comfortably either by your side or on your thighs. It might help if you can (if appropriate to do so) loosen any tight clothing around the wrists, waist or collar. Maybe kick off your shoes? All of these can be done when listening back to the audio when you relax, but for now we are just going to record your voice talking through the guided process of relaxation.

Be fully aware of any possible clenching of your teeth or fists or toes that is going on and allow them to relax.

You should now be ready to start recording. You can use any digital recording device such as a computer, ipad, phone or voice recorder. Don't increase your stress levels by putting yourself under any pressure to get it right first time you can always do another one. We will start with a very short process and as you get better at recording your own voice you can record longer ones at your leisure. You can even just read the text in your head without recording it to begin with until you feel ready to go to the recording stage.

As you are recording remember… you are speaking the text and not (whilst recording) trying to relax yourself. Maybe even, whilst recording, pretend that you are reading it to a stressed friend in an effort to help them relax and calm down.

Do not be concerned if you fall asleep whilst relaxing (I do this all the time….) and also do not be concerned if it does not work well for you at first (especially if you are a "high energy" person). Practice will make perfect.

Where the script suggests you say "breathe in", "breathe out", "hold that breath for a second" etc … allow a second or two to pause thus enabling the listener to take any requested action and for it to have effect.

Press record and begin to speak clearly word for word the following text;

In a moment you will begin a relaxation process. You will be safe at all times, and for any reason during the process, should you need to become alert and take action, you will be able to do so easily and normally.
Let us begin.
Take a long deep breath in and hold that breath for two seconds.
Slowly breathe out as you listen to your inner voice asking you to … relax.
Take another long deep breath in, holding the breath for two seconds and as you breathe out … relax further still. As you take further relaxing deep breaths, holding each breath for two seconds, feel free to allow your eye lids to gently close as you listen to your voice speaking to you, as you relax further still.
Long deep relaxing breaths, holding each breath for two seconds before breathing out and letting go of any traces of tension within your muscles, relaxing further still, with each breath more and more relaxed.
Give yourself permission to relax, telling your muscles to relax with each relaxing breath you take, noticing how good it feels as you relax further still.
Allow yourself to enjoy this feeling for a few moments ………

*(allow silence for 15-20 seconds or so)*Focus again now on your breathing. As you begin to take deeper breaths in and with each breath in you slowly, in your own time start to feel more awake, more alert and aware, and in your own time open your eyes and have a stretch.
Okay ….. Open your eyes, stand up, shake your arms out take a few deep breaths before returning to your day.

STOP RECORDING.

Now listen back to your recording but this time take part in the process allowing yourself to relax with the deep breathing etc.
If you took part in that exercise what you have just done is possibly lower your blood pressure slightly, allow a little more oxygen to disperse into the blood stream and release some tension from your muscles. Hopefully you managed to relax a little bit too?
The exercise that you have just taken part in is called a closed eye relaxation exercise, or sometimes "autogenics," at the end of this book we will do a full-length closed eye exercise (remember the first time you do it you will be recording it and not participating in it). You will then be able to go back to your recordings and follow the relaxation process at whatever time suits you.

How are you motivated? By a carrot or stick?

Just before I give you some more stress management and stress prevention techniques, let's just look at the consequences of you not preventing your stress.
I asked you to consider how you are motivated? Is it by a carrot or stick? Are you motivated to achieve something by that dangling carrot in front of you (the goal, the prize, the acclaim etc) or are you more motivated by the stick (I must do this or look what is going to happen to me)? This can vary from day to day and from situation to situation, as it can from person to person. We are all different.

Can you afford not to manage your stress?

It is important to understand how you are motivated because that can help you to understand the consequences to either preventing or not preventing stress. What are the consequences to you of not preventing stress and allowing it to control you? What could the impact be on your health, your physiology and your emotional or mental wellbeing? What are the consequences to you of not preventing stress at home or at work? How will it affect your finances, and your ability to achieve your goals in the future? How will it affect your family and your children or your friends around you? What are the benefits of you preventing your stress?

How much will that improve your home and personal life, your work life and relationships at work?

Think about the benefits of preventing stress on your health, the knock on effects on your finances, your ability and your wellbeing, which in turn enables you to go out and achieve your goals in the future. How much more energy will you have for your kids, your friends, your family around you? All of a sudden is it acceptable for you to "*not*" prevent stress?

Consistently applying the stress prevention techniques will lead to them becoming a habit and much … much easier to apply.

The consequences of "not" preventing stress lead to procrastination and a fear based "near" paralysis. Stress paralyses people into procrastinating, people can become afraid to make the most simple of decisions for fear of them being wrong.

All of this can develop into the four letter word we dislike the most … FEAR. Stress paralyses, and can lead us to enter a fearful state where decision-making becomes impossible. Taking action can then become impossible, in fact, it makes us want to just curl up in a ball and lay in bed all day. Have you ever been there? The consequences of both preventing and not preventing stress are there for all of us to see. The question is what you are going to do?

In the next section we will look at some other easy to apply prevention techniques. ….. like the one below.

Look into … not up to people.

In my business as a researcher and speaker for Stretch Development Ltd I am very keen on quoting information gleamed from a top achieving athlete and business-man by the name of Kriss Akabusi. Kriss is a gold medal-winning athlete for Great Britain and is a pretty well known celebrity in the world of television and professional speaking.
When I interviewed Kriss, he talked about how you should look *into* people and not look *up to* them. What I understood from this comment is that if somebody is really good at something and you want to achieve the same yourself, you shouldn't look up to them but you should look *into* them.
By looking *into* them you can understand how they think and behave, and by applying what you learn you yourself too can become more effective at that task.

Can you apply this strategy in preventing stress? Think about someone you know who is calm, stress free, excellent in decision making, great in taking action, and handling confrontation. Someone who seems to handle Christmas effortlessly and with a smile on their face from start to end. Why don't you ask them if you can take them out for coffee or maybe buy them lunch to get inside their mind a bit? Get some of their time, sit them down and ask them questions.

Some questions you may ask could be:
Will you share with me what it is you do that makes you more effective than others around you at managing your stress?
How do you think and behave when you notice that you are stressed?

What do you do to manage your stress?
What they tell you could make a *real* difference. Why?... because you are more likely to believe people who are able to manage their stress at the highest level so pick these people to *look into*.

Remember don't look up to, look into. Study them, ask them how they think and behave in stressful situations, ask them how they prevent and manage their stress and take action on what it is they tell you. Looking into can be the difference that makes the difference.

In this next section we will look at the twenty one day rule and how it applies to you in relation to you doing the things that will enable you to make lasting positive habits that will prevent stress.

Preventing Stress (Relaxation List)

It is a case of saying to yourself that you will do things that are the direct opposite of the things that cause you stress. Get a list of things (write them down) that you can do that are either free, cheap or if you have got lots of money, cost lots of money. This list needs to contain things you can do to make a difference … things that makes the difference for you.

You may need to start saving for some of them but for twenty-one consecutive days, I am asking you to consider filling a space in your diary with things you can do that are fun, relaxing and make you happy.

These things could include going for a walk through the park at lunchtime, helping someone else, or meeting up with old friends.
Is your stress related to something that happened a long time ago and there is somebody that you need to apologize to or maybe you need to give yourself permission to "let a person go" and release any hold that they have over your life?
How about going for a drive at the weekend to the nearest beach, lake or mountain, going for a walk to watch the sunrise or sunset, maybe spending time with your family, maybe sending someone flowers or filling your own home with flowers.

It might be just sitting down with a movie and a pizza, a great film, a bar of chocolate, having a chill-out night, maybe booking yourself in for a massage, cooking for friends or having someone cook you a meal.

You may decide to book a holiday and look forward to that or maybe treat yourself to a spa day. Either way, deliberately find things that you can do every day, put them in the diary for twenty-one consecutive days, find things that are opposite to those that stress you.

It's about saying *I will do this*.

One of the suggestions I gave above was to do a good turn for somebody else - help other people. Now for this gem of wisdom I must give credit to a friend of mine called Bryn Jones.

Bryn and I were both delegates on a training course when from nowhere he came up onto the stage dressed in a super hero outfit calling himself 'Captain Cadbury … a new breed of super hero'.

He started talking about wanting to make someone else's day and he then handed out boxes of chocolates to all the delegates saying, "I want you to be a super hero, I want you to be as open or secretive about it as you wish, but I want you to make somebody else's day.

I want you to go up to somebody who has done something over and above the call of duty, someone who has helped you by being "the difference that makes the difference to you" and I want you to thank them, give them the box of chocolate and notice their reaction.

Then, as you walk away, notice how that makes you feel. I challenge you". Well… the impact this had was amazing. Within twenty-four hours everyone was full of amazing stories about what had happened to them when they did this, how great it made others feel, and in return, made them feel **AWESOME!** Try it yourself a few times during your 21 days!

You do deserve to be stress free, you do deserve to look after yourself and have more fun in your life. This will help prevent stress. Make the twenty-one day rule happen in your life.

A German psychologist called Herman Ebbinghaus was a pioneer in work into memory, and he developed something called the curve of forgetfulness.

The curve of forgetfulness suggests that, after 21 days if you haven't consistently used information, you are less likely to remember it hence the curve of forgetfulness. Whereas, if every single day for 21 days you consistently apply the same information it becomes a habit and easily remembered and used. If you plan to start on the 4th December this year you could be totally in control by Christmas day. Why don't you use the 21 day rule and see what happens?

Anchoring a positive state of mind

Now we are going to look at how to anchor a positive state of mind. The term or expression 'anchoring' has been used in psychology and neuro-linguistics (NLP ... neuro linguistic programming) for many years. Anchoring, and the processes it uses however, have been used by human beings for thousands of years all over the world. Indeed you probably already anchor yourself, even though you may not even be aware you do it. If you were to walk out of here and find one hundred pounds on the street in a bundle, you would probably clench your fist and shout, "Yes! Fantastic!"

Well, ... really? ...explain. Think about very successful people. During a football game between England and Greece, the captain of England at that time was David Beckham. With nearly the last kick of the game he won a free kick from about 40 yards away from the Greek goal. The referee had the whistle to his lips to blow for full time, it was the last kick of the game, and David Beckham knew he had to score with this free kick, otherwise England would not be going to the European Championship finals. Talk about pressure and stress! He had 80 thousand people in the stadium going, "Go on Beckham, Come on Beckham!"

Millions of people all around the country watching their big plasma screen TVs going, "Go on Beckham, Come on Beckham!" I mean, goodness me…, can you imagine the pressure and stress, can you imagine that level of pressure?

David Beckham took the free kick, the ball curved through the air, just past the despairing fingertips of the diving Greek goalkeeper and hit the back of the net, England had got their goal and 80 thousand people went absolutely crazy. Millions of people, all around the country were celebrating, jumping up and down, hugging and screaming on the top of their voices …and in that moment do you think David Beckham went, "Yeah, it was alright, wasn't it?" whilst sauntering away whistling to himself? … or did he run screaming towards the corner flag sliding on his knees, clenching his fists, arms down by his side, shouting at the top of his voice, "Yeeeeeees!"? I think you know the answer! That is anchoring! – using a physical action combined with an emotional attachment to make a physical change in yourself. It is in a nutshell… taking control of your amygdala.

So, if top achievers anchor positive states of mind by running and screaming, "Yeeees!' and we only clench our fist and say "Yes" who's got it right, us or them? Now, don't be afraid, I am not going to ask you to go around shouting, "Yes!" and clenching your fists as people will think you're crazy!

If you're a student preparing for an exam and you are feeling a bit stressed, you can't stand up in the middle of an exam going "YES!!!!" just to focus your mind and have some energy because you will most likely get expelled.

If you are ready for a sales appointment, you can't stand in your sales appointment and go, "YES!" because you probably won't get the deal. However, you can control and trick your amygdala. We talked about the amygdala earlier it is the almond shaped mass of nuclei inside the brain that controls your emotions. To control and trick your amygdala all you have to do is think about the three most intense emotions that human beings experience. These are fear, happiness and love. These things tend to fool the amygdala and we can learn how to use these emotions to our advantage. If you are feeling ridiculously happy and for some reason you need to sabotage yourself and not be so happy (I can't think why you might have to do this but run with it…), all you have to do is think about something really fearful, something terrifying, and the amygdala is sabotaged. The opposite is also true. For example, if you are afraid or stressed and you think about something that makes you feel extremely happy, deeply loved or cared for your amygdala will be tricked and POW !!! you will feel better – especially if you attached *real* emotion to the thought and feeling.

Lets talk about happiness, because that is the most fun thing to do. Having said that, I think it is better to "be" happy rather than "do" happy? It is more difficult to do something than to be something. We can choose our responses in most situations so what if we were to "choose" to "be" happy? If we are happy then we will do things that makes us happy.

Think about the times when you laughed, so hard at something, that you couldn't contain yourself. Have you ever laughed so hard that your cheeks ache? Have ever laughed so hard that your jaw aches and you get tears in your eyes? Would you agree that after doing that for 40 seconds, you just feel great afterwards? Why is that? Here's why …..you feel great and your amygdala fires (takes action) when you experience intense emotions and adrenaline is released, neuro-adrenaline, serotonin, endorphin; all of the body's natural 'happy chemicals' are released into your system making you feel great. Ask yourself the next time you're stressed, to remember to anchor a positive state of mind, it must be better to have fun, feel good rather than stressed? You **can** control the amygdala if you don't it will control you. And you might say to yourself, "well I can't … or do not want to bring my arm down to my side shouting YES! loudly"

But you can actually make a choice to do this if you wanted to.

World champions of sports do it, so why can't or wouldn't you at least try it?.

Why don't you have a go right now?
What if it worked for you?
Again, only do this if it is physically safe for you to do so.
If you have any back, shoulder or neck challenges, do be safe and if in any doubt at all, go and speak to your doctor.
If for "any" reason it is not safe or appropriate for you to do this physically, you can still do it in your mind (visualising yourself doing it) as long as you really mean it and attach intense emotions to it as you do the process.
Just stand up in an area where you can stretch your arm out in front of you and turn around without hitting anything or anyone. Bring your healthier, stronger or preferred arm up and out in front of you at shoulder level.
Clench your fist and turn your hand so that your knuckles are facing the floor, and your wrist is facing the ceiling. Count to three and on "three", bring your arm sharply back to your side with clenched fist and tensed muscles in your arms shouting **"YES !!!"**
Try it again and **REALLY MEAN IT THIS TIME !**
Remember that the amygdala works better when the emotion is **BIG !**

A less physical "anchor" could be to play yourself your favourite music which is great and works well for many people, maybe have a bit of a dance? If you're sitting down and you are stressed, stand up, walk around, do some deep breathing, or do the closed-eye exercise you did earlier. Either way, anchor yourself a positive state of mind.

If you really fancy a giggle, why not get the whole family to anchor with a loud "YES!" every time something good happens this Christmas.

Deep breathing.

Anchoring can also simply be achieved by deep breathing. Keeping your eyes open, take a deep breath in, hold it for two seconds, and relax, let go of the tension in your muscles. Taking another long deep breath in, hold it for two seconds, and relax, just let go of any more tension that you can. Just allow with every breath out the muscles in your neck and shoulders to become more and more relaxed. Just release that tension.

Power napping

What if you were to agree with your family that in order for you to be at your best, you would ask for twenty to forty minutes where you can go to a quiet room or place and have a little nap? Relaxation is like power napping. Do you remember the power napping concept from the 1980s? People used to power nap. It really works, why don't you try it? Just take yourself off for five minutes and do some deep, head to toe closed eye relaxation. If you're afraid of falling asleep, set an alarm on your watch, phone or computer to beep at you to wake yourself up. If you do fall asleep that means you really are relaxing yourself.

You can anchor yourself by thinking about the best moments of your life. Play your favourite music, think about your first kiss, passing your driving test, succeeding in an exam, maybe for you it's your wedding day that works or the time you achieved that job you always wanted. Maybe, it's a certain smell that makes you feel good.

Remember the smell of doughnuts at a funfair and candy floss? Some people use the smell of freshly cut grass to feel relaxed but if like me you suffer with hayfever, maybe that is one to avoid! For many it can be a taste such as allowing a cube of rich velvety chocolate to slowly melt in the mouth.

Remember the taste of jam doughnuts. How about sounds? For some people it is the sound of, let's say, waves lapping on the seashore or a childs' laughter. For some people its accessing emotions of deeply cared about things, people and places. Either way, pick whatever is best for you, use something that you can consistently apply as an anchor, something that works for you.

Your book of inspiration

In this section we're going to talk about your book. Now, your book is different to a book that you can buy. You could pay a lot of money to have your book produced or alternatively you can do it very cheaply with an old photograph album and some picture cuttings.

This concept was first introduced to me by a gentleman called Reg Athwal. Reg is a professional speaker based in Dubai and when meeting him, he showed me the book that he had made.

Reg looks at his book before he gives a presentation as it helps him to relax and make himself feel great.

Reg had used a photograph album in which he had put pictures of things that meant the most to him; things that he achieved, his friends, his family, places he'd been, the things that had happened that were great in his life as well as pictures of things he wanted to achieve.

The book also included letters and testimonials from people who said really great things about him.

How do you think you would feel if you created a book like that for yourself and any time you were going through a stressful situation, or before you went into a stressful situation, you sat down for three to four minutes and just flicked through the book allowing yourself to feel great?

I can promise you, since doing this for myself, it's been a difference that makes the difference. I beg/challenge you to do it. Go and get an old photo album and put into it photographs of people, places, things that you love or are very proud of, things that you have achieved. In my book, I have got pictures of me standing on mountain tops, doing a fire walk, swimming with sharks, my son, my wife etc.

All the things that I have done that I am proud of are in that book. The letters, the quotes, testimonials on the networking sites, the nicest things that people have said about me have all been put into this book. Why don't you do it? …

Why don't you do it?

Another idea for using a book is to get one of those folders that have clear pockets for each page so that you can put in each sleeve things each Month to remind you of great things you did that Month.

Maybe in January you went to the cinema and had a massage and you kept the receipts? Maybe you took a photo of you out on a walk or giving flowers to an elderly neighbour? If each Month you did this, you could sit on Christmas morning in bed, maybe with a glass of something fizzy, and go through each Month/sleeve and remind yourself of the great year you have had.

Buddy Up !

Another strategy that you could try is to find somebody else who might be in a similar place as yourself in regards to their levels of stress. Ask them if they would like to 'Buddy Up' with you which will enable you to support AND hold each other accountable at times of stress over Christmas and new year to make sure that you are applying these techniques so not allowing yourselves to get too stressed.
You could agree that if you see each other getting too stressed that you give permission to your buddy to tap you on the shoulder and say "hey… why don't you try….?"
You could go for coffee each week, twice a week or even every day if you had to, or maybe text, call or Skype each evening to keep each other on track.

Going Rhino !

How about trying to go Rhino with your stress?! I have to pay tribute to the best selling American author called Scott Alexander whose first book "Rhinoceros success" has changed the lives of so many people (including my own). Scott uses some very simple positive psychology with a humorous twist by suggesting that we can either behave like cows or rhinos.

We can either, be a cow, and shy away from taking responsibility for our goals, health, wealth and happiness and choose to hang around with the same type of people (other cows) who end up being driven by other peoples goals and intentions for us, or we can be Rhinos… who see what they want and have a good old

CHARGE!

The danger is that we tend to behave like, and become like, the people we associate with the most, and so by definition, if you hang around with people who are sucking the life blood from your very existence through their negativity (other cows), then we as a result are far more likely to start "moo-ing" with the herd.

 I have heard these people called all sorts of things ranging from mood hoovers to energy vampires and much worse besides.

Think for a moment …….. at home or work are you aware of spending time with those who gossip, whinge and moan about almost everything? Do you need to step away from the herd and go rhino a bit more? Gossip …. or go!

Sometimes, if we want to change and those around us will not allow us to, or do not wish to change themselves, it is a hard fact but sometimes we have to let these people go and move out of their circle of influence in order to enable ourselves to develop and grow.

The exact same can be applied to situations or people that affect our levels of stress.

Many of us do not like the thought of letting people go, especially if they are close to us (friends, family, work colleagues etc) but if they will not change, or if we can not change them, we must face facts in that by making a choice to stay in that situation we are BY CHOICE choosing to accept the stress that goes with that. If you have a potato that has a small bad section within it, we do not throw out the whole potato but we do "cut out the bad". If we did not cut the bad bit out, and left it, it would grow until the whole potato became bad. We MUST step away from those who bring us down. By saying this I am not referring to those who need our help, support or compassion, but to those who delight in bringing everyone else down in mood, and maybe even cause issues simply to avoid moving forward.

Identify the cause of your stress and take responsibility for sorting it out. Even "things" can have a cow hold on us at times. In modern society at times many of us can (or should) admit to being sedated by watching too much television or shopping for things that we simply do not need. In my view, the biggest drain of peoples' energy and self determination in todays world can be the internet and social media. I have seen too many people who are drawn into its lure and they waste "too many" hours of their life in a meaningless stream of communication that serves to achieve little if anything at all. It can lead to sleep depravation, eyesight issues and much worse.

The Power Hour !

If I have been working away a lot, I can sometimes return home to a desk piled high with notes, actions, letters, parcels, papers, bills, invoices, messages and reminders. I can be easily overwhelmed by such things and whilst I know that I "should" crack on for a few hours and clear the decks to start work with a clear mind, I tend to push it to the end of my desk and add to the pile over the next day or so.

I know…. that this is bad. But it is not as bad as one day when cleaning my office I saw a piece of paper under the desk that had a great enquiry on it.

I picked up the phone and called the potential client only to hear how, because I had not got back to them quickly enough that they had gone elsewhere when they were going to book myself.

How about once a week you have a power hour where you prioritise your jobs (or pile of papers) and then just hit the ground running and plough through them not being distracted by calls, emails or other well intentioned people who have their own agenda for your time, energy and resource? See how much more you can get done in that hour.

For personal stress prevention (rather than managing stress once it has arisen) why not set your mobile phone to silently vibrate on an hourly alarm?

Place the phone in a pocket or on your desk nearby so that you feel and hear the phone vibrate, and when you do notice this happening, stop what you are doing and take a few seconds to deep breathe, relax, walk around or do something to lighten your mood. Other people will not do this for us, and so it is up to us to take responsibility for ourselves.

Reaching Out

It can be hard to talk to others about how you are feeling but to do so is a sign of strength and to not ask for help or support can be counter productive. At work, if your bosses do not know that you are stressed they cannot do anything to help you or relieve what it is that is causing your stress. They can only help if they are aware.
If your level of stress and emotional distress is such that you feel unable to talk to friends, family or work colleagues then maybe it is time to visit the doctor and ask for their help and advice.

Laughter

Having a good laugh can make every day a better place to live in. Yet, so few of us plan to have a laugh. We would rather sit late at night watching new and current affairs or political based programmes that fill our heads with negative events and confrontation, rather than make a deliberate choice to listen to, read or watch something funny.

What if the family agreed that over Christmas you would not have your phones or Facebook on, maybe not watch any news or depressing documentaries, and instead filled your spare time watching things or doing things that made you SMILE or laugh?

My wife and I, over the last year made a decision to get out more and laugh more and as a result we have seen some awesome stand up comedy. It even led to me delivering some stand up comedy myself at an open mic night …… if you can call what I did comedy!

Laughter is a super fast broadband connection to your bodys' natural happy chemical cocktail. The rush of endorphins, and the release of oxytocin driven by laughter can make almost any stressor fade into the distance as you laugh away your cares – even if the relief is temporary. Go on …. Have a giggle !

Music

 For many of us, music can be a powerful motivator, but few of us use music for more than idle pastime. In schools I have noticed more and more schools doing away with the bells and alarms, and replacing them with music that gently gets louder (or softer) which prepares the mind for lessons or break-times and gives everyone including the teacher time to get ready for the start or end of a class or break-time rather than the silence that is pierced by the shrill claxon or alarm.

How about replacing your alarm clock with a mood clock that with 5 minutes prior to your get up time begins very quietly to play soothing or uplifting classical music as a light slowly gets brighter? Bedtime with these clocks can be equally as relaxing as the light slowly fades out to a gentle piece of music that relaxes you to sleep.

If you play an instrument, why not plan to play every day if only for ten minutes. Many people find that when they are focused on playing an instrument it is near impossible to be stressed about the other things at the back of your mind as your brain focuses on the task in hand of creating music.

Singing is also a superb way of changing a negative "state" by getting oxygen flowing and working facial muscles (regardless of how good a singer you are … or not).

There can be nothing better than belting out a song at the top of your voice to make you feel happy. How many times have you pulled up at traffic lights to glance across at the car next to you to see somebody giving it their all as they belt out their favourite song that has come on the radio? Ask yourself this question…… do they look happy or stressed? Go on…. I dare you! (but do watch the road eh).

Dancing to music can also really relieve stress so whether you are a dancer or not, and I am not (I am built for comfort, not speed), why not put on some tunes and boogie like nobody is watching you.

Or … maybe go to dance classes and have a date with your friends or partner?

Either way, music is a cool way to let go of the stresses of life.

Closed-Eye Relaxation

Okay... We've looked at the causes, effects, symptoms, and consequences of stress and looked into many stress prevention techniques that you can easily apply to make a difference to your life. The closed eye exercise is however one of the biggest things you can do to reduce your stress.

Remember, as described at the beginning of the book, first time around to record yourself (if possible) speaking the process so that when you want to relax, you can hear "your own voice" telling you to relax. During this exercise, again, please do not operate machinery or drive. If you suffer with epilepsy, please keep your eyes open throughout this exercise.

The closed eye exercise is an autogenic process where you will relax yourself, from head to toe. You are going to imagine your muscles relaxing from head to toe and then at the end of the process you will energize yourselves and comeback feeling great. What I want you to do, is either lie flat on the bed or floor or sit in a comfortable place; your legs and arms should be uncrossed and your limbs not touching each other, by that I mean your arms should be just slightly away from your body and your legs slightly apart.

If you're sitting in a chair, please sit in a straight backed-chair with your back flat against the back of the chair and your feet planted firmly on the ground. Please rest your arms either by your side or on your thighs, whichever is most comfortable for you and whether you are lying or sitting, please be aware of whether or not you have your hands drawn into fists, toes or teeth clenched, and if so relax them.

Think about whether you have any particularly tight clothing around your waist, wrist or neck and if so please loosen them. Be aware if you are clenching or grinding your teeth in which case just allow your jaw to relax. If you need to be awake at a certain time, just in case you fall asleep, please set an alarm on your phone, watch, computer or on a clock close by so that if you need to you can be woken up at the time that you need to. If at any point you need to open your eyes for any reason, you're able to open your eyes and be alert and wide awake and be ready to be safely and fully in control at any moment.

Remember …. Read through first and then record the process before you apply for yourself, the process for relaxation.

This next process is longer than the first one. Again... If you suffer with epilepsy, please keep your eyes open at all times (of course you may blink), and if your condition is anything more than very mild, or if you have "any" medical condition that might not be suitable for this process, I would strongly suggest that you consult your doctor before doing any closed eye relaxation process. This includes, but is not limited to, heart conditions, blood pressure issues, emotional or psychological challenges, lung or chest health issues or fits/seizures of any type. For everybody else, the outcome will be far more beneficial when you close your eyes when you listen back to the audio I am asking you to record.

PRESS RECORD:

Be aware of your breathing. Is it very shallow from high in the chest or are you breathing very deeply from down in the pit of your stomach? Just be aware of your breathing.
I would like you to take control of your breathing and be more aware of your breathing.
Notice what you notice, as you take control of your breathing and you start to take long, deep breaths, with each breath, just holding that breath for one or two seconds before breathing out and allowing yourself to let go of tension in your muscles ...... and relax.
With every breath out, allow yourself to become more and more relaxed.

With each breath, allow yourself to relax still further, releasing any last traces of tension particularly around the neck and shoulder area. Remember that at any time, or at any point, you can safely open your eyes and be alert, awake and respond to any situation that requires you to do so.

But for now, continue taking several long deep breaths, giving yourself permission to relax further still and allow your eyes to gently close if you wish, as you relax further still.

In a moment, we're going to count from five down to one.

Continue taking long deep breaths with every number we count just allow yourself to relax further still.

Give yourself permission to float and drift deeper into a safe, comfortable state of relaxation.

Five:

Imagine the muscles on the top of your scalp and forehead just relaxing, releasing tension as you now drift deeper and deeper into relaxation.

Four:

Feel now the muscles around your cheek bones and the back of your head and neck and your chin relaxing.

With every breath, breathe out releasing tension and all the facial muscles relaxing further still.

Floating down further, giving yourself permission to relax further still as the muscles around your shoulders relax.

Three:

Further now, more relaxed with each breath out, the top of your chest, your upper back and down to the stomach towards your waist, around your sides and lower back…. With every breath out, feel more and more relaxed.

Two:

Further on down… and down, drifting, floating into a safe place of total relaxation, releasing the tension from the muscles in your waist, your bottom and your thighs.

One;

Take a longer deeper breath and hold it for three seconds and as you breathe out just allow a wave of relaxation to flow from your head down to your thighs removing any last traces of tension, relaxing you still further.

With your next breath, down your thighs around your knees and your calf muscles and shins.

With your next breath, down around your ankles floating down further still, relaxing, drifting, giving yourself permission to release the tension in your muscles.

Give yourself permission to allow a moment or two to enjoy your safe, relaxed state.

(allow silence for 20-30 seconds or so)

Focus again now on your breathing as you begin to take deeper breaths in and with each breath allow yourself to feel a little more awake.

In a moment we are going to count from one up to five and with each count you will take in a long deep breath, enabling more oxygen to get into your body and then hold it for two second allowing yourself to feel a little more alive, a little more alert and a little more awake.
One,
Take a long deep breath in hold it for two seconds, allow yourself just to become more aware of your surroundings.
Two,
Take another long deep breath in holding it for couple of seconds and just begin to have a little bit of a stretch maybe tense the muscles a little bit in your arms and relax them again.
Three,
Take another long deep breath.
Maybe start wiggling your toes, moving your mouth and your facial muscles……… just put a bit of life into them and become increasingly aware of your surroundings including noticing the seat or the floor beneath you and just become increasingly alert, alive and awake.
Four,
Take a long deep breath in, prepare to gently open your eyes on the count of five and with further breaths just allow yourself to feel more alert, more awake and energised.
Start moving your limbs, maybe have a little stretch and be prepared on five to open your eyes and in your own time when it is safe for you to do so, stand up and have a bit of a stretch, returning fully energised, alert and awake.

Five,
open your eyes, give yourself a smile, and in
your own time, when it is safe and comfortable
for you to do so, have a little stretch, maybe a
walk about and go back to your day feeling
refreshed.

PRESS STOP:

You can now, in your own time, go back and
listen to your audio recording of that process and
fully engage with it to help with your stress
prevention. Practice makes perfect - both for the
recording and the practice of relaxation.
With practice over twenty one days you will be
able to make this relaxation a very positive habit
and within seconds with practice you will be able
to relax from head to toe in just three deep
breaths. Remember never to use machinery or
drive whilst recording or using a relaxation
process.
I hope you enjoy the closed eyed relaxation
process, hopefully it will be a great
demonstration of how you can take control of
your physiology and relax yourself from head to
toe.
You will find that with practice and dedication
over a period of time the process gets easier and
more and more affective especially if you have
sleep troubles (especially getting to sleep

When we experience periods of ongoing stress, we can be tempted to turn to things that comfort us. These perceived comforts can range from the seemingly sublime things such as chocolates, confectionary, sugar based products, flowers, through to the more "less than appropriate" things such as maybe a whole bottle of wine (rather than a glass) or recreational drugs be they over or "under" the counter.

The effect of excess alcohol and/or drugs on the system actually causes the system greater stress as it tries to manage the toxins that are being put into the body.

Therefore, a better way to manage or prevent stress is to drink water, eat some fruit, go for a brisk walk, do some gentle exercise, or deep breathing.

The endorphins, serotonins, adrenaline, neuro-adrenaline and oxytocin that are created by doing these things will have far better and healthier impact on your well-being and levels of stress in the longer term than the initial "left hook" of perceived gratification from indulging in alcohol or drugs.

Tensing and clenching

Another quick and effective strategy of tensing and clenching really works for some people. if you have any (even mild) blood pressure issues I would strongly recommend you seeing a doctor before trying any clenching or tensing. The tensing and clenching strategy in principle comes from a theory shared with me by a phenomenal professional speaker called Peter Roper. Peter encourages people to tense a certain part of their body which in turn actually forces other parts of the body to become slightly more relaxed.
This works as it's much harder to be really tense numerous parts of the body at the same time. So for example if you clench a certain part of the body (and my colleague suggests the buttocks) .... Yes!!!... I know this sounds silly but if you were to stand up straight and clench your buttocks for just a few seconds (as long as it's healthy and safe for you to do so), hold that clench for about 5 - 6 seconds, and then relax you might notice that other parts of the body are not as stressed as they were before.

The same will happen if you tense other parts of your body that were previously tight when you release the tension you should find that they are not as tight as they were before.

To relax try either doing the buttock clench or the slower but more thorough process of tensing and the relaxing all your muscles by working from your head down to your toes.Have you considered going to meditation or relaxation classes or meditating/ relaxing at home?
If you decide to have a go at home go onto You Tube where you will find dozens and dozens of videos that you could watch and relax along with. If you prefer audio programs there are plenty that you can download from iTunes to help you understand and learn how to meditate and/or relax yourself. I would strongly suggest that you try this. Find one that you like and that works for you and keep doing it. It is making these things a habit that will move you from managing stress to preventing it in the first place.

Getting things in perspective.

At times of severe stress, it is very easy, and sadly not constructive at all, to focus on yourself. You can at times find yourself focusing on how you feel, the effect the stressful situation is having on you and those around you and/ or the stressful situation itself (work, personal life, finances, health etc).

Sometimes focusing on other people and other situations equal to, or maybe even worse than your own can take your mind off your own situation and perhaps at times make you realize that other things are just maybe more important than the thing you were previously worrying about.

Doing this helps us to grab a sense of perspective and "truth" around our situation.

I remember having more than a few troubles in my mind and life when I interviewed an amazing woman that, despite her challenges, limitations and "very real" adversity, had achieved a truly amazing amount of things in her life that made me place my issues into perspective. Since that time I have rarely, if ever allowed myself to wallow in that level of self pity and if I do I only have to think of that amazing woman and my challenges seem very small.

Do you know somebody like this who could maybe help to put your own challenges into perspective?

What if you dedicated Christmas this year to looking after somebody on their own or in need of friendship or a little time?

We all can, but how many of us will I wonder?

Showing gratitude

Have you ever considered showing gratitude as a form of stress relief? Showing gratitude for the things that you've got?
If you have a roof over your head, a bed to sleep in and a wardrobe to hang your clothes in, you are still in a minority of humans on the planet that have these basic commodities. How amazing is that fact? We can go into a total meltdown if we do not have internet connection or our phone drops signal, yet many people around the world still fight a daily battle for clean water and a safe place to rest their head at night. How about if you were to get a pen and paper and list all the things in your life you currently are truly grateful for? These could be very big things such as family, friends the fact you are healthy, alive, the fact you have a roof over your head and a bed to sleep in. Maybe you have a job meaning that you can live comfortably, or they could be very simple things such as "I am alive".

Either way, what is it you need to show with gratitude for, and how much more of a "cool world" would this be if we all acknowledged this to ourselves and others? A friend of mine (Steve Houghton-Burnett) has started a movement online where he encourages people to actually list their gratitude's online?

(see http://theformulaguy.com/personal-growth/a-million-gratitudes)

Have you considered going one step further by doing something tangible to help other people so enabling you to take your mind off what you are stressing about? Some people I know are huggers They just love hugging people. If you are lucky enough to have someone in your life why don't you ask for a hug? Why don't you grab a hug? Why don't you give a hug? Take your mind off your tension.

How about listing the things that are causing you stress and asking yourself what are the key things here and are there any similarities? (remember security, acceptance and control). Are there any issues you've listed 'your' interpretation of what is true, if so ask yourself are they indeed actually true? Focus on the things that *you can* take responsibility for right now, look at each one individually rather than trying to work on two, three, four or even five things at once. Completion (and success) is better than mediocrity. Once you have picked one thing that you can take control of take action towards it so that it can be removed from your stress list.

During periods of great duress and anxiety sometimes we can feed that anxiety by concentrating on it too much and giving that thing, that situation (or person) far too much of our time, energy and resource. I wonder what would happen if you were to pick on something positive in your life and give that thing as much, if not more, time and energy and resource? Surely it can be more beneficial? So focus on the things *you can* take responsibility for and take massive, positive action towards achieving them.

For example … communication. We've all received written communication, voice messages or had meetings with people (be they friends, family or work colleagues) where somebody has said something and we have interpreted it differently to how it was "meant" to be. Maybe somebody has said "well of course people do X, Y and Z !" and we interpreted it as they were "having a go" at us. Maybe our wrong interpretation of this led us to get really stressed about it, and led to us challenging them about it, and this challenge turned into an argument? When in actual fact they were not referring to us in this context at all! Maybe it was us who said the thing that was heard and received in a way that was not quite how we meant it…. And as a result, relationships were challenged or even broken?

So what should we do?????????

Instead of falling asleep in front of the Queens speech or the James Bond movie this Christmas day, or falling out over the game of monopoly, what if in the afternoon you took it in turns to share what you are truly grateful for in life?

Always find out what is true in a situation.

Allow me to give you a personal example. I am a person that (at the time of writing this) could do with losing more than a little bit of weight and being a lot healthier. Due to travelling a lot, having a demanding schedule and other "excuses" I use, it is true that I tend to eat not only too much, but also too much of the wrong foods.

I believed that I really liked these foods, however, once I discovered how great I feel when I find out some facts about what I am eating and change to foods that are better for me my "truth" changed.

My truth changed to the extent that twice a year I love to have a de-tox period where I juice fruit and vegetables, eat fish and white meat, and lots and lots of salad and vegetables. I try to cut out as much as possible of the salt, sugar, and processed food that I give into so (and too) easily the rest of the time.

After starting this I always feel so much better but before I start I am more than aware of a huge resistance within me to making that first giant step towards positive change because I crave the salt and sugar loaded foods.

As we have said earlier sometimes stress can be caused by an overload on our system by eating too much and drinking too much of this stuff (the wrong things), and they should be consumed with moderation only.

Now I am as yet not in a position to lecture anybody on healthy eating but merely suggest this because our "version" of what is true can all too often be off course, not entirely true, and in some cases, so far removed from the truth that we need a wake up call.

If you go onto you-tube once again there are many hundreds of videos that can suggest the different ways that a person can eat and prepare food more healthily, but I always recommend that you go to a health professional for advice in the first instance if you are in the least bit concerned.

Here is something that most of us need to do. Gaining a little knowledge and understanding of what are safe levels of salts; sugars and fats within our most common food intake can change our shopping, cooking and eating habits. Look at the contents of some of your favorite foods, especially the foods you turn to for comfort when under duress.

There are numerous, and easily accessible surveys and bodies of research that explains (some in too graphic a detail) what happens to our bodies when we put carbonated drinks, sodas and pop inside us because of the levels of sugar, caffeine and other chemicals that they mix the drinks with.

Consider doing a partial de-tox, look "into" juicing and introduce it slowly to your diet regime and if in doubt, always seek medical advice before starting any diet regime.

Consider especially if you are a drinker of alcohol, cutting down on the quantity you drink and moderating the regularity of your drinking. If you are taking drugs (pharmaceutical or recreational) for solace or comfort, seek professional support in coming off drugs or lowering the dose and strength of the drugs to have a lesser impact on your physiology and well-being.

I once saw an exercise on the effects of a cigarette on our insides. It was delivered in my old high school by the then head teacher and he had an old fashioned set of fireplace bellows used to create a draft to ignite an open fire. He placed a lit cigarette in the front nozzle, covered the air hole of the bellows device body with a balloon and pumped away at the bellows with this lit cigarette in its end until the cigarette had been smoked down to its filter.

In effect, the bellows had smoked the cigarette. When it had finished he said, "Later today I will cut open the balloon and the filter of this cigarette put it in a glass case on the wall in the reception area of the school for those of you who smoke to see what you are putting inside you EVERY TIME you smoke a cigarette."

It was **horrific;** the filter was full of an obnoxious looking and smelling orange-brown coloured stain. The balloon inner was coated with what appeared to be a dark foul smelling and looking syrup. I can assume it would have been the tar and nicotine from the cigarette.

I would not want to think that every cigarette that I was at that time smoking was pumping that rubbish into my system but the truth is that it probably did. That practical and somewhat graphic exercise shocked me to my core.

I smoked for a while after that, but far less than before and later, stopped altogether and whilst I still, from time to time, quite fancy a cigarette, I have not been tempted to start again. This was thanks to that exercise. Do you need to be told a "home truth" about things you are doing to yourself? Who needs to do that in order for you to listen to it? Friend, doctor, family member, son, daughter, partner?

I know people who do smoke when stressed and they habitually take a long inhalation of smoke with their first few intakes of smoke, and they breathe out again with an almost sigh of relief that they are letting go of the stress they are experiencing … but their body is actually going into stress to deal with what it is the person is smoking.

Surely that can't work as a plan? We trick ourselves into thinking "ahhhhhh that's better" when in fact we should be saying "will this cigarette (replace with what ever your crutch is; drink, food, cigarette, workload etc) serve me or poison me?"

Resentment is like drinking poison and expecting somebody else to die – Peter Thomson.

Have you had any ill feeling or negative thoughts about another person or maybe even a gift you received (or did not receive)?

What if instead of wasting another minute of your valuable life in resentment you asked questions of the other person to see if your assumption is true or not? Work with what is true. The worst that can happen is that you establish that you were right.

The best scenario could be that you have a laugh at yourself for wasting so much time and energy on a wrong assumption.

Deep breathing

Online it is possible to find many different courses, workshops, training or instructional videos on how to practice deep breathing and stretching exercises to help you to relax more.

I have worked (and played) amongst many cultures around the world where the stretching/yoga/tai-chi/morning exercises they practice contain breathing and stretching exercises as they are known to produce tangible and measurable health benefits for those who take part.

I remember in Beijing, China looking out in a morning at the parks, and even central reservations in the middle of busy roads, where I could see large groups or individuals taking part in stretching, deep breathing and tai-chi exercise before they started their days' work.

How about this evening before you lay down to sleep, you put a reminder on a piece of paper by your alarm to remind you not to leave the bedroom the next morning until you have done some of these?

Try and do some mild gentle stretching exercises, and maybe some deep breathing exercises.

If this has any positive effect for you do it again tomorrow, and the next day, and the day after that until it becomes a habit that serves you, rather than the usual wake up, coffee, work routine.

If it does not serve you or has a detrimental health or well-being impact on you stop doing it, at least you can say you had a go.

It is far better for you to test a number of these ideas to see if they work rather than dismiss them out of hand. At times it can be far too easy to dismiss new information or health supporting ideas offered to us but, if we try and open our minds and take responsibility, it is becomes easier for us to try different things that maybe we were previously closed to, enabling us to find ones which work for us and ones which don't.

Keep doing the ones that do work and make them part of your daily routine or regime. Build them into the diary by allocating time in the day for a little exercise, a little stretching and a little deep breathing.

Prayer, faith and worship

I am going to have people shouting at me for this but being blessed to know so many people from all over the world with such cultural and religious diversity, I see one common thread.

FAITH !

It seems to not matter what or who they have faith in, but rather the act of faith that binds so many people together. Their faith enables them to find solace, comfort and strength at times of hardship and emotional distress.

If you hold little or no faith, I am sure that you can find something or somebody to have that "feeling of unconditional love" for. Maybe it is a child, a place or a good and true friend or life partner.

For many though, regardless of the religion involved, it is their God to whom they turn when times get tough. The act of prayer can be relaxing and soothing by itself.

Even a scoundrel may be found speaking to his or her God when they are in their darkest hour. Prayer can be a refuge… if you let it. Why not take some time to engage with your God at a deeper level than maybe you have done of late?

Worry

Worry can lead to stress, and for some personality profiles worry can take over and prevail every thought. A sad fact is that most worry is self-determined and assumption based, and therefore is frequently "not true". Why would we do this to ourselves?

Well, for some people it can be used to re-enforce patterns of behaviour that they want to prevail or need to prevail because it affirms who they "think" they are, instead of "knowing" what is true about themselves.

Allow me to give a few examples here. You may or may not be able to associate with one or more of these and those will appear quite rational to "you" and the others that do not apply will appear quite irrational.....

The mind reader – this is when we jump to conclusions and attempt to mind read a situation by saying thing like "I just know it is going to fail" or maybe "I know that the boss hates me".

The reality check – "I have just watched a scary movie, and I feel scared, and so this means I should be afraid in case I am in danger right now"

Perfection or failure – "it must be perfect or it is all wrong and useless"

The one thing – "the day was full of joy and happiness but that one comment ruined the whole day for me"

Win or bust – "we lost one match and so the whole season is doomed to failure and we will not win any games now"

Dismissing positives – "it wasn't me", or "it was nothing really", or maybe "I got the job but that was only because the rest of the applicants were so poor"

Worst case scenario – "some people do not have car insurance so I just know that somebody without insurance is going to crash into me"

Should do-ing – beating yourself up over things you "should have done" or "should be doing"

The "I can't" label – "I did not pass my maths exam and so I just can't do maths".

NLP – Perceptual Positioning or… The umpires exercise.

I got myself trained as practitioner of NLP (neuro linguistic programming). NLP is a study of our communication skills and effectiveness traits.

Within my training I was trained in and became a huge fan of an exercise that I have since called the 'umpire exercise'. The umpire exercise enables you to take a situation which you need to resolve and in your minds eye, relive the situation.

Using your imagination you imagine two chairs facing each other in front of you, one for yourself and a second chair for the other person involved in the issue that needs resolving.

The situation (that potentially is causing you the stress and anxiety) which needs resolving is then replayed as if you and the other person are sitting down and having the conversation that caused you stress. If it is a "perceived" situation rather than a situation that has actually occurred, imagine the other person and imagine how the conversation might go.
For this exercise I would ask you consider an event that "has" happened that needs resolving.

You need to relive the situation in fine detail in your mind seeing what was going on, hearing exactly what was being said, and what was "really" implied as opposed to what we may have "assumed" was implied etc.

In the left hand chair you set an exact clone of yourself and in the right hand chair is an exact clone of the person you are talking to.

This exercise is a pragmatic exercise and is not to be taken lightly. It can reaffirm your belief about a situation or person, or it might challenge your assumptions in a profound way.

This technique can offer solutions to a situation that previously you might never have considered possible. It is about seeing things from all sides… a devils advocate position if you wish to think of it that way.

The idea of the umpire exercise is that you view the conversation from a totally neutral perspective, which I confess at times, can be hard to do when emotions are high. Consider it a small test of ones emotional intelligence. You are 'the third person' or 'the umpire'.

As the umpire or the third person you "*have" to be impartial*. By using this technique you have the benefit of seeing both persons' body language, facial expressions, eye movements, gestures, you can hear more clearly the tonality of their voice and the speed of their speech and therefore this additional information will enable you are to grasp a greater understanding of the situation.

It may enable you to consider more as to the other persons 'true' intent when the situation is being replayed rather than when the situation was happening for real, and your emotions were so heightened and maybe….. just maybe…. we may have not been listening 100% to what was being said or how it was being said because we were too busy preparing what we were going to say as soon as they just "SHUT UP AND LISTENED TO ME !!!!!".

You watch the conversation playing out and remembering that as the umpire you **HAVE** to remain impartial. Notice the way the clone of "yourself" responds to the other persons words.

Are you showing yourself in the best light? Are you making any assumptions about the situation? … the other person?.... their "intent"?... or the words being said to you?

Look at the other person, are they being as challenging as you think or are they trying to get you to understand their side? Are they making assumptions based upon your reaction, tonality or body language?

See, hear and experience the situation from a neutral perspective and then as the umpire in your head give both characters feedback on what you saw and what you heard.

Then you step into the other person (the person causing you the stress or anxiety) and you go through the scenario again in your mind but this time 100% from their perspective as if you are wearing their shoes. Living the situation with them, trying to get their point across to you.

Of course you will be in some cases making up in your head what it is they are thinking but if you know the person even reasonably well you can probably gauge in this situation what their "true" intent really is.

And if it is to cause you stress then you have a greater understanding of that situation, but... what if it isn't? What if you can sense a rising level of frustration that is causing things to be misunderstood?
Is this response clouding the other person's ability to comprehend the point that it is you are trying to make?

When the conversation is played out in your head tell the other person (you) and the umpire how you experienced that situation from the other person's perspective.

Repeat the exercise a third and final time but this time through the perspective of yourself in the first chair. Notice this time how you're sitting, how your head is positioned, the volume and tonality of voice, whether you maintain eye contact or look away, your body language, use of gesture, or not as the case might be. Are we giving the person the respect that they deserve?

Maybe, …. maybe not.

Only you know what is true and *that* is what is important. In this exercise, it is too easy to go through this exercise from a position of, "Well I know what's going on" or "I know what they really meant".

To be honest, is to be gracious, even if the outcome is not necessarily the one that you wanted or expected. It may be that as you go through the situation one last time, you still have the same opinion of the situation or the other person that you previously held.

That sometimes is the case for me. However so many times I do this umpire exercise and ask the other person to give me feedback in my head, and realize that maybe I didn't communicate in a way that I intended and maybe I didn't respond to their words in a way that I was proud of.

Maybe I allowed myself to hear what I needed to hear or understand what I needed to understand in that situation.

Allow the umpire to give feedback to both parties and then reflect on the exercise and ask yourself what is it you need to do. If there is something different you need to do, go and do it.

There have been many times I have ended up going away from doing this exercise where previously I had wanted to argue, challenge or confront the individual over a stressful situation, but after listening to my umpire I actually ended up going to that other person with a sincere apology and then asking them to explain again.

This time as they explained to me I listened with both ears fully open and asking for clarification if I thought I had misunderstood anything.

Effective communication can prevent problems and reduce stress.

The question is, are we big enough sometimes to notice when we need to listen more, apologize more and take responsibility for our responses within a communication with another?

Making sure we have understood a person's intent rather than trying to 'mind read' the situation and the intent from the other person is only a good thing.

A simple checklist for yourself;

1. Check yourself.

Are you reading a situation correctly and are you responding appropriately to the situation? Are you hearing and understanding things as they "should be"?

2. Listen to other people within that situation, listen to the other person rather than make assumptions about the others intent and do ask questions to seek clarification and understand very clearly. If the other person is still saying things that you really disagree with, make sure you get their opinion in writing so there are no opportunities for misunderstanding. If there's the opportunity to listen to other people externally to this conversation (audio recording – with permission) and indeed if it is appropriate to do so, maybe get another person's opinion.

3. Finally, you then talk. You speak to the other person. If it is that you believe you are in the

right, speak clearly, use simple language and make sure you explain what it is you wish to put over, and what is not acceptable to you within that situation.

There is no need to raise your voice, to be rude or to be the antagonist. If the other person chooses to raise their voice, be rude or antagonistic then that is a clue for you to determine whether or not you want or need to be around that person.

I've met so many people who are stressed out about people and situations in the workplace and yet all they have to do is leave and find a working environment and a company that deserves their skills and talents.

Unfortunately too often they are afraid to leave.

Stress displacement – letting it go

Finally I would like you to think about displacement of stress and anxiety.

Displacement can be used in many ways. I have seen different ways of managing displacement of stress be it physical, mental or emotional. I have seen people use anchoring (as we discussed earlier in this book), I have seen people use hypnosis, relaxation, and any number of techniques to remove, reduce and manage their stress.

One of the more effective things I have experienced myself though, is something called the 'Sedona Method' (there's lots on the Sedona Method on the internet).

The Sedona Method is a very simple process of asking yourself a handful of quality questions.

Questions about your response/s to a situation.

Frequently we try to push down our feelings as a means of us "not dealing with them", especially in the western world where we (in some extreme cases) would rather end our lives than deal with our biggest challenges.

Not dealing with our stress can lead to a, build up of emotions which in turn will begin to crowd our thoughts and thinking (even when trying to relax).
Sadly, if this is stress is not dealt with, it can cause physical, emotional and mental unrest, and if left unchecked can eventually lead to ill health.

When you are doing the Sedona method the idea is to displace, move or ideally remove the stress or anxiety by asking yourself three questions, and taking action on your emotional, mental and physical being.

The questions are;

Could you let that go?

Would you let that go?

When?

Lets have a go…

Let's think about a situation, which it is causing you some anxiety or stress.

It may be a situation that over time, you have become aware that when you think about it your shoulders (or other areas of your body) tense or it is taking too much of your thinking time.

Consider question number one, … could you let that go?

In theory, if you were able to let go of this unhelpful thing,… you would. But "could you"? For most people in "most" situations (NOT ALL) you "could" let go of your attachment to this thing.

You might not want to though, as you may hold some attachment to feeling angry, stressed, anxious, resentful, bitter, sad, twisted, but most people will say "I could but I don't know how, … but in theory, yes I could let that thing go."

There are very few exceptions where people are not ready to let go. These situations are typically associated with severe distress and anxiety and maybe where the individual been abused, or people are not ready to let go because they have an attachment to that "thing" be it mental, emotional or physical.

To some who have experienced intense trauma or adversity, it can feel like they believe it to be a part of their identity.

It can feel like it is part of their make-up, and is part of who they are as human beings. This is not true.

For these people it is highly recommend that professional counseling or therapy is found to help them come to terms with that situation.

However most of us, in the cold light of day, could let go of those feelings even though it is hard to do. So in "most" cases, yes, you "could" let go.

So now you move over to question number two. If you could let it go ... would you let it go?

In the pragmatic cold light of day, if its something that is causing you stress if you could let it go, why wouldn't you let it go?

How could it possibly serve us to "hold onto" unhelpful thoughts and feelings? Now it sounds too simplistic, but if you could let it go, why else would you want to hold onto it? How does it possibly serve us or benefit us by holding onto stress, anxiety, resentment, and bitterness?

So if you could, (in most cases) you would. If at this stage, anybody is resistant to letting go, it is possible they will be better served by working with a therapeutic professional.

Number three, … when?

If you could let it go, and therefore, would let it go, when will be a good time to let it go?

Now? in an hour? how about tomorrow? next week? next month? next year? why not now?

Because if you could let it go, and you want to let it go, why not let it go .. now?

So the Sedona Method takes people through these questions and even guides them to a place where they are prepared to let go.

Using the Sedona Method you can take yourself on a visual process in your mind where you can imagine certain parts in your body where stress is manifesting itself.

For most of us, we can identify with this statement. Many people get headaches, there are those for whom the tension is in their necks or their shoulders, their back, their sides, maybe their stomach churns, maybe they just a "grouch", for everyone it could be different.

Where does the stress tension manifest itself within you? For example if I felt that my shoulders were tense, I would imagine visually the tension in my muscles and I would allow it to be there.

Yes… that is right. I would give it permission to be there. If that seems counter-productive then do please read on.

I would turn the tension into an imagined object, a thing, something tangible that I can control. I would give it a shape, a colour, and I would take control of it. This is critical; **you** take control of the stress, the tension, the anxiety.

So as an example, even though there is not an object in my shoulders causing me stress, I would visualize that stress as (for example) an orange ball.

I would say the orange ball is still, maybe it's small, maybe it's large, maybe it's not still, maybe it's turning slow or fast, maybe its bright orange, maybe it's a dull orange.

It matters not to start with as long as you accept whatever your creative mind creates for you, and you notice what it is.

I would place all of the stress that I could mentally, visually, emotionally and physically focus on, into that ball, so that "the ball" becomes the thing that is causing the stress, and then I would take control of it.

I would control it and make it do the opposite of what it is doing at the time for example I would stop it from turning, I would shrink it down and turn it to a dull orange.

By doing this I have taken control of it, all the tension, all the stress, all the anxiety in that ball is now under my control.

I would then imagine the ball moving from my shoulder blades, across my shoulder and down one of my arms, past my elbow through my forearm and as it reaches my wrist I would clench my fist.

I would imagine placing the orange ball visually inside my fist and then I would clench my fist tightly so that after a while it's difficult to comprehend where my hand ends and the ball begins due to the level of intensity with which I are clenching your fist (being sure not to actually hurt myself doing so).

Then I would ask myself the questions, could I let that go?

Of course I could.

So you say, "Yes, I could let that go."

If I could … then would you let that thing go?

When?

And I would say, "Now."

As I say "now", I take a breath in, hold it for two seconds and as I breathe out I just release the tension in my fist as I lower my hand or arm to my side I imagine the ball visually dropping out of my hand and rolling away into the distance getting smaller and smaller until it disappears.

It seems a crazy exercise but, if you take part fully in that visualisation process, what you do is displace the source of your stress by putting the energy of that stress, the anxiety, the situation, the tension from you into an object and then remove the object/stress from your person.

Psychologically, emotionally and mentally, you have displaced the stress. With practice, and by using the three awesome "Sedona" questions with deep breaths and letting go of the tension, you can really master this method.

It was first taught to me by an expert on the subject of emotional intelligence, a guy by the name of Sanjay Shah based in the UK.

There are Sedona practitioners all over the world, so if this exercise appeals to you and has any measurable value or benefit when you have tried it a few times, why not track one of them down and ask for a few expert facilitated sessions?

Conclusions

The stress prevention techniques within this book can give you the certainty, confidence and conviction to take control of your stressful situations so that you can prevent stress, using fun and easy to apply stress prevention techniques.

We have looked at the way top achievers prevent stress and how you can understand the causes, the effects and symptoms of stress.

We looked at the consequences of you taking action …or not, in relation to stress.

We have looked at control, security and acceptance and some of the main causes of stress and how the CSA can affect or be the reason behind these things.

We looked at anchoring, we looked at the use of "your book", and we considered the twenty one day rule using simple and "easy to do" things that every day in a small way, can help to make you happier and more stress free.

You have read about looking into people who have great relaxation and stress prevention stress methods that you could possibly model.

We have also recorded and practiced the closed eye relaxation process that with time can be a superb daily routine to keep you on top of your game.

I hope you took great benefits from the closed eye relaxation exercise and that you listened to your recording over and over again to make sure it becomes a habit for you.

Stress prevention can be achieved and you deserve it. You do deserve to be stress free and I look forward to hearing how you have used these techniques to create more energy and well being for yourself.

For more information on stress prevention training or our other workshops please go to

www.stretchdevelopment.com

www.davidhyner.com

Thank you for reading,Bye-bye for now.

Printed in Great Britain
by Amazon